Sports

for Kids age 1-3

By Dayna Martin

1

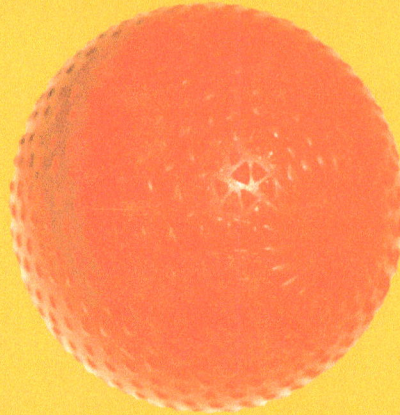

e ENGAGE BOOKS

Mailing address
PO BOX 4608
Main Station Terminal
349 West Georgia Street
Vancouver, BC
Canada, V6B 4A1

www.engagebooks.ca

Written & compiled by: Dayna Martin
Edited & designed by: A.R. Roumanis
Photos supplied by: Shutterstock & iStock

FIRST EDITION / FIRST PRINTING

LIBRARY AND ARCHIVES CANADA CATALOGUING IN PUBLICATION

Martin, Dayna, 1983–, author
    Sports for kids age 1-3 / written by Dayna Martin ; edited by A.R. Roumanis.

(Engage early readers : children's learning books)
Issued in print and electronic formats.
ISBN 978-1-77226-095-3 (paperback). –
ISBN 978-1-77226-096-0 (bound). –
ISBN 978-1-77226-097-7 (pdf). –
ISBN 978-1-77226-098-4 (epub). –
ISBN 978-1-77226-099-1 (kindle)

1. Sports--Juvenile literature.
I. Roumanis, A. R., editor
II. Title.

GV705.4.M37 2015   J796   C2015-903418-3
                                    C2015-903419-1

Sports

for kids age 1-3

Engage Early Readers

Children's Learning Books

by Dayna Martin

ENGAGE BOOKS / VANCOUVER

3

Baseball

4

Basketball

Soccer

9

Volleyball

Tennis

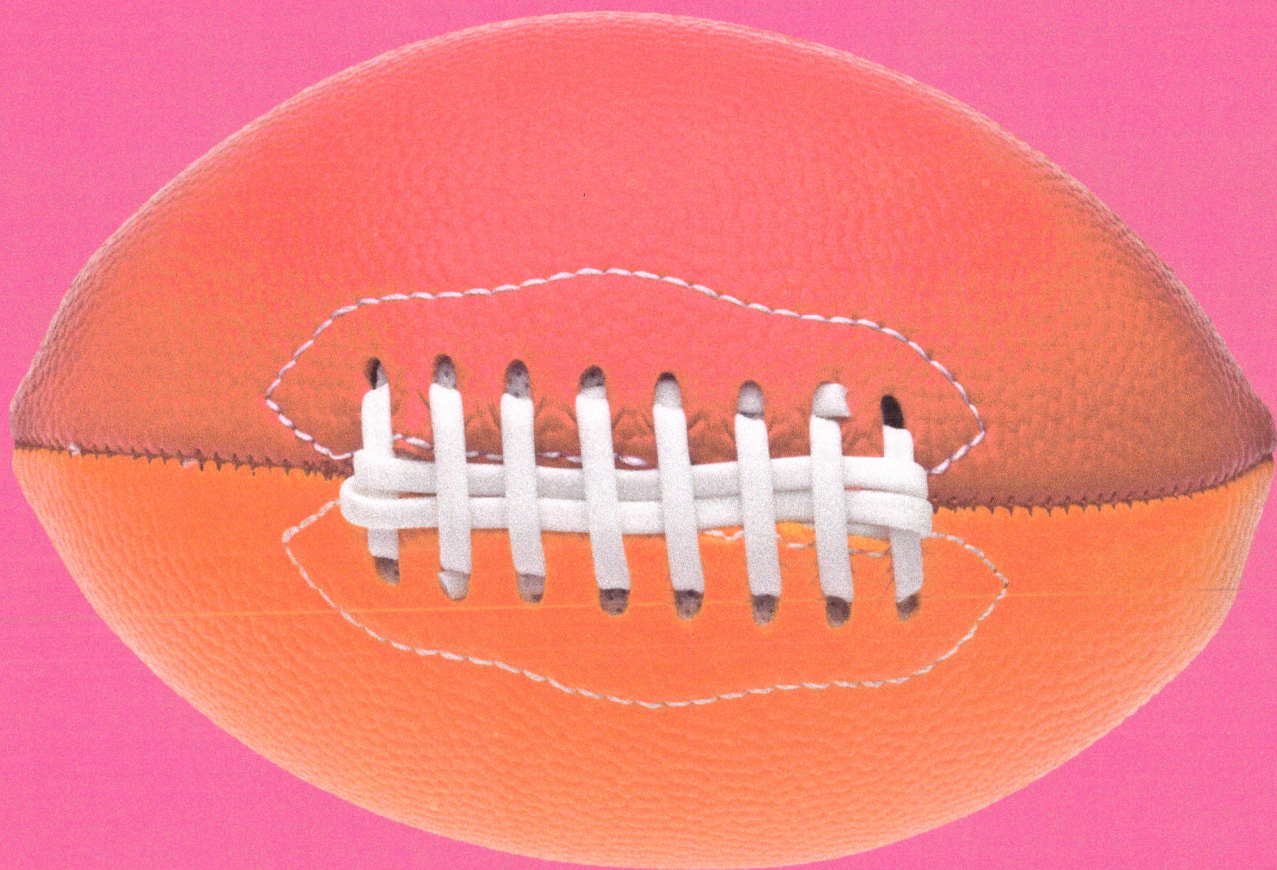

Football

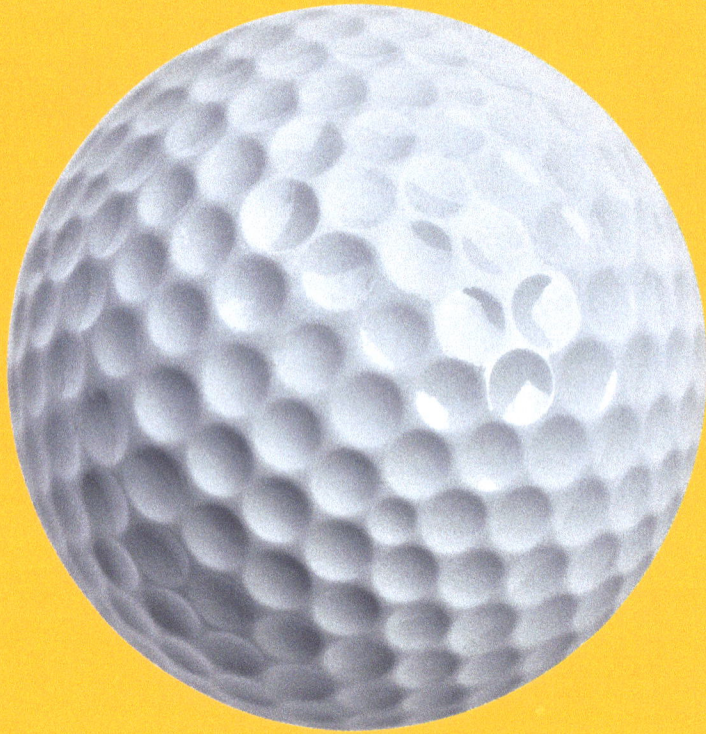

Golf

17

Hockey

19

Softball

21

Badminton

Lacross

24

Water polo

Billiards

Ping pong

28

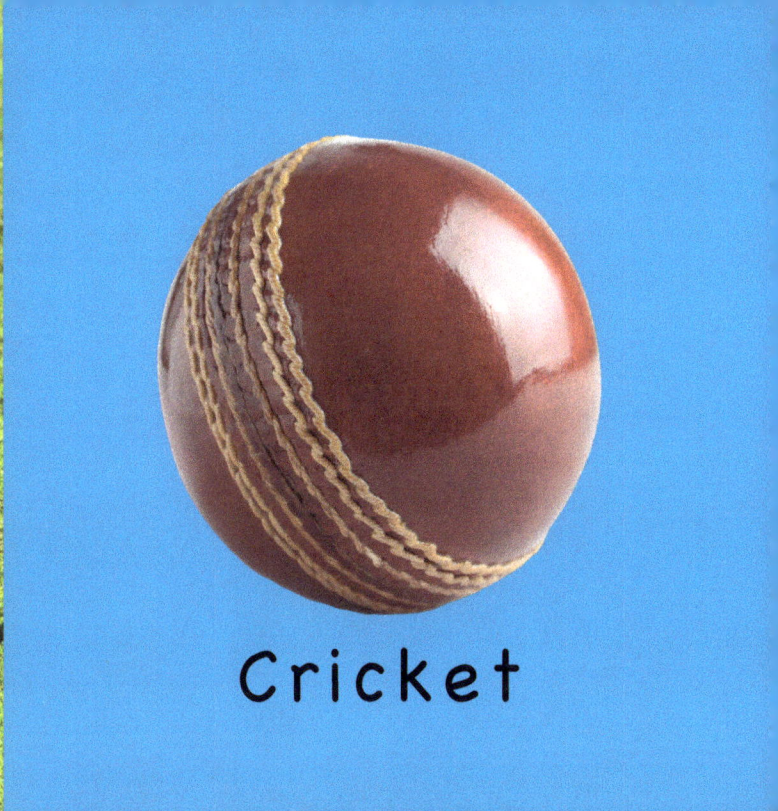

Cricket

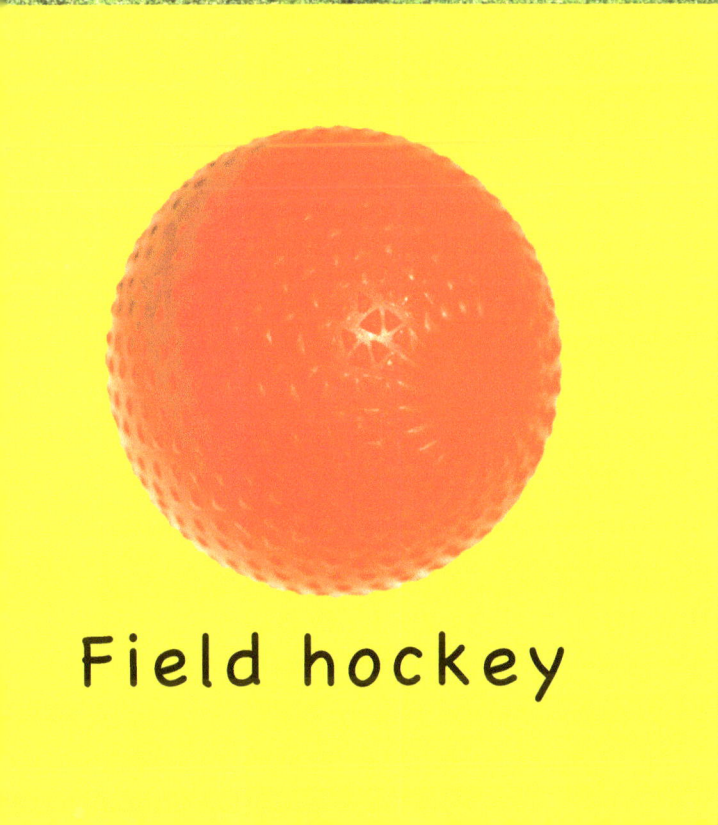

Field hockey

29

Sports activity

Do you know what these sports are called? Can you find **basketball, golf, football, soccer, baseball, hockey, badminton, tennis,** and **volleyball**? Match the names to the pictures below.

Answer: football

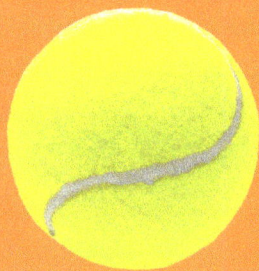

Answer: tennis

Answer: hockey

Answer: baseball

Answer: basketball

Answer: soccer

Answer: golf

Answer: badminton

Answer: volleyball

For other books in this series visit www.engagebooks.ca

age 1-3
colors
for kids

Yellow Fish
Orange Flower
Purple Eggplant
White Bear
Red Fire Hydrant
Blue Hat
Pink Pig
Green Lego

age 1-3
Opposites
for kids

In
Out
Long
Short
On
Off
Up
Down
Big
Small
Slow
Fast
Front
Back
New
Old

age 1-3
Actions
for kids

Eat
Jump
Crawl
Brush
Wave
Kick
Swim
Ride

age 1-3
Sizes
for kids

Small
Medium
Large
Small
Large
Medium
Small
Medium
Large
Large
Medium
Small
Medium
Large
Small
Large
Large
Medium
Small
Medium
Small

age 1-3
Numbers
for kids

4 Raspberries
7 Rubber Ducks
2 Cars
8 Presents
5 Cups
1 Bowl
6 Balloons
3 Pickles

age 1-3
Emotions
for kids

Bored
Silly
Proud
Shy
Brave
Grumpy
Fear
Shock

age 1-3
Shapes
for kids

Starfish
Clock
Leaf
Chalkboard
Door
Rings
Cracker
Pizza

age 1-3
Sounds
for kids

Ribbit
Moo
Vroom
Flush
Clap
Ring
Roar
Cock-a-doodle-doo

age 1-3
ABCs
for kids

Fox
Lion
Vulture
Tiger
Bear
Rabbit
Dog
Cat

www.ingramcontent.com/pod-product-compliance
Lightning Source LLC
Chambersburg PA
CBHW051311020426
42331CB00020B/3499